A Penny Saved

By Pam Zollman

CELEBRATION PRESS
Pearson Learning Group

It is good to save your money.
There are many reasons to save.

Something you want might cost more than you have. If you save your money, you can buy it.

week one
25¢

week two
25¢

week three
25¢

week four
25¢

TOTAL $1

If you save your money, you will have money when you need it.

When you want to give a gift to someone, you can buy it.

Some people save their money in a bank.

inside a bank

A bank is a safe place to keep your money.

outside a bank

Save your money so you will have it when you need it.

A Penny Saved

By Pam Zollman

CELEBRATION PRESS
Pearson Learning Group

It is good to save your money.
There are many reasons to save.

Something you want might cost more than you have. If you save your money, you can buy it.

week one
25¢

week two
25¢

week three
25¢

week four
25¢

TOTAL $1

If you save your money, you will have money when you need it.

When you want to give a gift to someone, you can buy it.

Some people save their money in a bank.

inside a bank

A bank is a safe place to keep your money.

outside a bank

Save your money so you will have it when you need it.

A Penny Saved

By Pam Zollman

CELEBRATION PRESS
Pearson Learning Group

It is good to save your money.
There are many reasons to save.

Something you want might cost more than you have. If you save your money, you can buy it.

week one
25¢

week two
25¢

week three
25¢

week four
25¢

TOTAL $1

If you save your money, you will have money when you need it.

When you want to give a gift to someone, you can buy it.

Some people save their money in a bank.

inside a bank

A bank is a safe place to keep your money.

outside a bank

Save your money so you will have it when you need it.

A Penny Saved

By Pam Zollman

CELEBRATION PRESS
Pearson Learning Group

It is good to save your money.
There are many reasons to save.

Something you want might cost more than you have. If you save your money, you can buy it.

week one
25¢

week two
25¢

week three
25¢

week four
25¢

TOTAL $1

If you save your money, you will have money when you need it.

When you want to give a gift to someone, you can buy it.

Some people save their money in a bank.

inside a bank

A bank is a safe place to keep your money.

outside a bank

Save your money so you will have it when you need it.

A Penny Saved

By Pam Zollman

CELEBRATION PRESS
Pearson Learning Group

It is good to save your money.
There are many reasons to save.

Something you want might cost more than you have. If you save your money, you can buy it.

week one
25¢

week two
25¢

week three
25¢

week four
25¢

TOTAL $1

If you save your money, you will have money when you need it.

When you want to give a gift to someone, you can buy it.

Some people save their money in a bank.

inside a bank

A bank is a safe place to keep your money.

outside a bank

Save your money so you will have it when you need it.

A Penny Saved

By Pam Zollman

CELEBRATION PRESS
Pearson Learning Group

It is good to save your money.
There are many reasons to save.

Something you want might cost more than you have. If you save your money, you can buy it.

week one
25¢

week two
25¢

week three
25¢

week four
25¢

TOTAL $1

If you save your money, you will have money when you need it.

When you want to give a gift to someone, you can buy it.

Some people save their money in a bank.

inside a bank

A bank is a safe place to keep your money.

outside a bank

Save your money so you will have it when you need it.